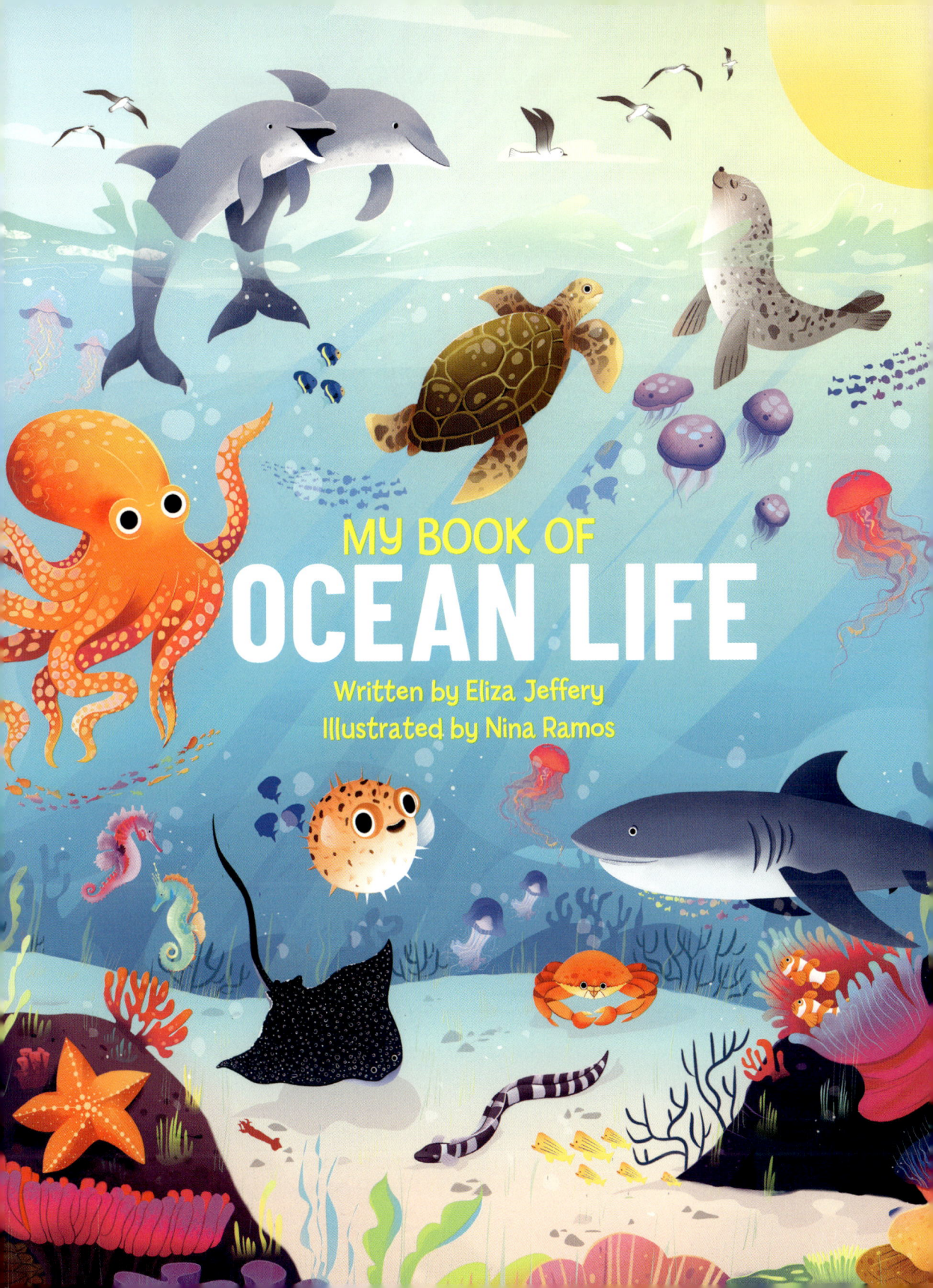

CONTENTS

Ocean Life	4
Coral	6
Jellyfish	8
Octopus	10
Sea Turtle	12
Sharks	14
Penguin	16
Rays	18
More Great Ocean Life	20
Keeping Oceans Healthy	22
Glossary	24

Copyright © 2026 Hungry Tomato Ltd

First published in 2026 by Hungry Tomato Ltd
F15, Old Bakery Studios, Blewetts Wharf, Malpas Road, Truro, Cornwall, TR1 1QH, UK.

No part of this publication may be reproduced, stored in a retrieval system, or transmitted in any form or by any means, electronic, mechanical, photocopying, recording, or otherwise, without prior written permission of the copyright owner.

A CIP catalog record for this book is available from the British Library.

ISBN 9781835694435

Manufactured in the USA

Discover more at
www.hungrytomato.com

Words in BOLD can be found in the glossary.

OCEAN LIFE

The ocean is MASSIVE!

The ocean covers most of our planet. It is home to some wonderful creatures of all shapes and sizes. The oceans are important for helping all animals to survive. There are five different oceans around the world:

ATLANTIC OCEAN

The second-largest ocean in the world. There are lots of interesting **species** in the Atlantic Ocean, including sea turtles and dolphins.

PACIFIC OCEAN

The largest and deepest ocean in the world. The Pacific Ocean is home to the Great Barrier Reef, the largest coral reef in the world!

ANTARCTIC OCEAN

The most recently named ocean in the world. The Antarctic Ocean is home to 17 different penguin species.

ARCTIC OCEAN

The smallest ocean in the world. In the Arctic Ocean, you will find a variety of species, from polar bears to whales!

INDIAN OCEAN

The Indian Ocean covers a large area of the world's surface. Lots of marine animals swim in these waters, including rays and sea turtles.

CORAL

coral has been on Earth for 240 MILLION YEARS!

Coral may look like pretty rocks and plants but it is actually an animal! It stays in one place during its lifetime and becomes a home for lots of other sea creatures. When coral grows together, it's called a coral reef.

Tentacles to catch its food

JELLYFISH

Some jellyfish can GLOW IN THE DARK!

They have bag-like bodies and tentacles that can sting other animals. Jellyfish have no eyes, heart, bones or brain! They are **transparent**, meaning you can see through them.

Jellyfish are mostly made of water.

A jellyfish sting can be painful for humans!

Jellyfish can be different, striking colors, like pink, yellow, blue, or purple!

DID YOU KNOW?

I eat... plankton, plants and small fish.

I can be found in... deep and shallow water.

I live in a group called... a smack.

My babies are called... ephyras (eh-fear-as).

OCTOPUS

An octopus has EIGHT LEGS and NINE BRAINS!

They have no bones, which means they can squeeze into tight spaces. Octopuses can squirt ink to scare away **predators** that try to eat them, like whales and sea otters!

Octopuses have three hearts!

SEA TURTLE

Sea turtles have been around since the DINOSAURS!

Female turtles come ashore to lay eggs on the beach. As soon as the eggs have hatched, the young make their own way to the water without any help!

Sea turtles can put their heads into their own shells!

SHARKS

Sharks are FAST SWIMMERS!

They have an excellent sense of smell that helps them hunt **prey**, even when it's really far away. They have no bones in their body but plenty of teeth!

Hammerhead sharks have flat heads so they can feed on flat prey, like stingrays!

Sharp teeth for catching and eating prey

Sharks are at the top of the ocean **food chain**.

Powerful tails to swim quickly and smoothly through water

DID YOU KNOW?

I eat... seals, fish and sea lions.

I can be found in... deep oceans and coastal areas.

I live in a group called... a shiver.

My babies are called... pups.

PENGUIN

Penguins can survive in VERY COLD places!

These birds can't fly, but they are very strong swimmers. They can hold their breath for up to 20 minutes when diving underwater for fish.

Male penguins look after the eggs.

RAYS

Rays are very CLEVER HUNTERS!

They use electrical signals to hunt their prey. Unlike most fish, rays have teeth to help them crush shellfish. They have no bones in their bodies.

Long tails to whip predators with!

Large fins to push themselves through the water

DID YOU KNOW?

I eat... shellfish and worms.
I can be found in... shallow water.
I live in a group called... a school.
My babies are called... pups.

MORE GREAT OCEAN LIFE

There are so many fascinating animals in the world's oceans to learn about. How many of these animals have you seen in real life?

SEAHORSE

Seahorses don't have stomachs or teeth - they suck their prey in through their snouts! They eat plankton, shrimp and small fish. Seahorses can make their bodies black, brown or yellow to hide from predators.

Seahorses live in groups called herds.

They can be found in warm, shallow water.

Baby seahorses are called fry.

Seahorses use their tails to hold onto things so they don't drift away!

SEAL

Seals are very playful creatures and live in groups called herds. They can hold their breath underwater for up to 2 hours. In fact, they can sleep underwater!

A mother seal knows her baby just by its smell! The babies are called pups.

They can be found in coastal and open waters.

Flippers help them to swim and catch fish easily!

CRAB

Crabs have exoskeletons, which means their skeleton is on the outside of their bodies. They have ten legs, two pincers and an egg-shaped shell that protects them from predators.

They can be found in rockpools and oceans, although some prefer **freshwater habitats**!

They eat seaweed, clams and small fish.

Crabs live in groups called casts.

KEEPING OCEANS HEALTHY

Our oceans are VERY IMPORTANT!

The oceans face many difficulties, but there are ways we can help prevent these problems and take care of our oceans.

CARING CORAL

You can save water in lots of ways, like turning off the faucet while you brush your teeth! This keeps the oceans at the correct levels, allowing coral reefs, and all the ocean animals and plants that live there, to thrive.

KEEPING TIDY

Make sure that litter is put in the correct bins so that it doesn't end up in the ocean! Plastic in the ocean can get stuck on animals like sea turtles and jellyfish. Animals also eat plastic because they think it's food. This can really harm them.

LEARNING MORE

Talk to friends and family about all the amazing creatures that live in the ocean, and why we need to protect them! The more people who are in the know, the more people who can help!

GLOSSARY

Camouflage - something that blends in with its surroundings so that it's difficult to see.

Coastal - an area of sea or ocean that is close to land.

Food chain - a way of showing how each animal gets its food.

Freshwater habitats - places with natural water that doesn't contain salt. It is found in rivers, ponds and lakes, but not in oceans.

Predators - animals that hunt and kill other animals for food.

Prey - animals which are hunted by other animals as food.

Species - a group of living things that are the same as each other. For example, hammerhead sharks and great white sharks are different species.

Transparent - something that you can see clearly through.

Webbed feet - toes that are connected by a thin piece of skin. Some animals have these to help them swim.